D1710217

SHAPE YOUR OPINION

Do Kids Need Year-Round School?

by Carolyn Williams-Noren

NORWOOD HOUSE PRESS

Norwood House Press
P.O. Box 316598
Chicago, Illinois 60631

For information regarding Norwood House Press, please visit our website at:
www.norwoodhousepress.com or call 866-565-2900.

Hardcover ISBN: 978-1-59953-931-7
Paperback ISBN: 978-1-68404-203-6

Library of Congress Cataloging-in-Publication Data

Names: Williams-Noren, Carolyn, author.
Title: Do kids need year-round school? / by Carolyn Williams-Noren.
Description: Chicago, Illinois : Norwood House Press, 2018. | Series: Shape your opinion | Includes bibliographical references and index.
Identifiers: LCCN 2018004330 (print) | LCCN 2018003231 (ebook) | ISBN 9781684042104 (ebook) | ISBN 9781599539317 (hardcover : alk. paper) | ISBN 9781684042036 (pbk. : alk. paper)
Subjects: LCSH: Year-round schools--Juvenile literature. | School year--Juvenile literature.
Classification: LCC LB3034 (print) | LCC LB3034 .W55 2018 (ebook) | DDC 371.2/36--dc23
LC record available at https://lccn.loc.gov/2018004330

312N—072018
Manufactured in the United States of America in North Mankato, Minnesota.

Table of Contents

Most kids in the United States have nine months of school and three months of vacation.

1

What's the Argument about Year-Round School?

Almost all schools in the United States are open for around 180 days every year. School starts in August or September. Students go to school from fall to spring. School ends in June. There is a long vacation during the summer. Most schools have used this calendar for many years. But some have tried a new idea: year-round school.

What Is Year-Round School?

Does year-round school mean kids never have a day off? No. Most year-round schools have 180 school days every year. That is the same as in a regular school. But these schools don't have one long vacation. Instead they have many short ones.

One example is Piedmont Elementary School. It is in Charleston, West Virginia. Students go to school for nine weeks. Then they have a three-week break. In summer, the break is a little longer. It lasts four weeks. The breaks between school **terms** are called **intersessions**.

During intersessions, kids might work on special projects in small groups.

What Happens during Intersessions?

Sometimes, the whole intersession is a vacation. Kids and teachers don't go to school. Instead, students may stay at home with their parents. Some may go to day care or camp. Others might travel with their families.

Some year-round schools have special intersession programs. School is open, but students don't go to their normal classes. Instead, they go to special classes.

At Piedmont Elementary, some intersession classes help students who are having a hard time. Other classes give kids a new challenge or a fun subject to explore. These classes are called **enrichment** classes. Regular school days may not have time for these activities.

The number of year-round schools is growing. In 1985, there were only around 500 year-round schools in the United States. In 2007, there were around 3,000. In 2012, around 4 percent of all public schools were year-round schools. That's 3,700 schools.

Year-Round School Calendars

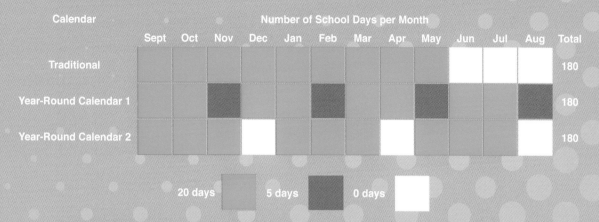

Calendar	Number of School Days per Month												
	Sept	Oct	Nov	Dec	Jan	Feb	Mar	Apr	May	Jun	Jul	Aug	Total
Traditional													180
Year-Round Calendar 1													180
Year-Round Calendar 2													180

20 days   5 days   0 days

This graph shows a nine-month school calendar and two types of year-round school calendars. Each calendar has the same number of school days. The school days and breaks are spread out differently through the year.

In Favor of Year-Round School

Some people think that more schools should switch to a year-round calendar. They say that year-round school helps kids learn better. They say students and teachers enjoy school more. And they say it would not be too hard to change schedules.

Many families go on vacation over the long summer break.

Against Year-Round School

But some people disagree. They say changing the calendar does not help students learn. They think a long summer break is important. And they say that changes cause problems for businesses and communities.

EXPLORE THIS BOOK

In this book, three questions about year-round school will be examined. *Is a long summer break good? Does year-round school help kids learn better? Is changing to year-round school worth the trouble?* Each chapter ends with a section called **Let's Look at the Opinions**. This section focuses on points to remember when forming an opinion. At the end of the book, students can test their skills at writing their own opinion essays.

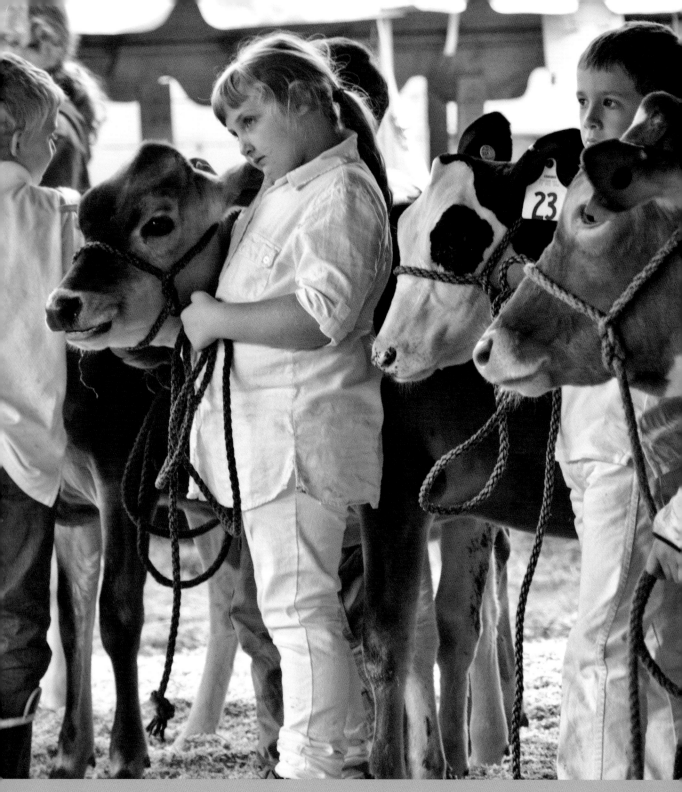

Farm kids today still help with animals and crops during the summer, but fewer people are farmers.

2

Is a Long Summer Break Good?

NO: Long Summer Breaks Aren't a Good Fit for Today's Families and Schools

A long summer break has been a **tradition** in schools. But why? Many people say it started when most families lived on farms. Summer is a busy time for farmers. Kids had to help with the crops and animals.

In most families today, all of the adults have jobs. This leaves nobody to take care of the kids all summer. Child care can be very expensive. In some families, kids go to camps or fun classes.

But these activities often cost money. Many families can't afford them. Some kids spend the summer home alone.

Long Breaks Are Not Used Well

It may be hard for kids who are home alone to use their time well. They don't always choose to play outdoors, read books, explore, and learn. Instead, they might eat junk food and play video games too much. This can be bad for their health.

It's true that breaks are important. But many short breaks can be better than one long break. Rick Loy is a principal of a year-round school. He says short breaks lead to better student behavior. He explained, "I haven't had one student sent to

On a long break, kids might choose to play video games all day instead of being active.

the office all week. And I know why. We've just had two weeks off, everyone is refreshed."[1]

Summer vacation is a tradition. There are lots of good things about it. Families enjoy travel and other summer fun. But year-round schools still have time off in the summer. And family traditions can be changed to fit the new schedule.

YES: Kids and Teachers Need Rest, and Summer Is the Best Time

People say that summer vacation comes from farm life. But that isn't true! Kenneth M. Gold studies history. He learned that summer vacation began in cities. It did not start on farms. There were many reasons for a break. People believed rest was important. Leaders wanted to give students and teachers a long break. Rest and breaks are still important today. So summer breaks should continue.

Summer break can be a time for kids to explore on their own.

Long summers are a part of life for American kids. Many people think of summer vacation as a time of freedom and fun. Without summer break, these traditions would be lost.

Hot Weather and Learning Don't Mix

Summer also isn't a good time to be in a classroom. The weather is hot. Many schools don't have air conditioning. Have you ever tried to sit still and pay attention in a hot, stuffy room? If you have, you've seen summer isn't the best time for learning.

Many schools are not prepared for summer heat. When classrooms are hot, students find it hard to learn.

DID YOU KNOW?

Today's school years usually include 180 learning days. In the past, students were in class for more days. In 1842, students in Detroit, Michigan, were in school for 260 days!

Summing It Up!

People have strong feelings about this issue. Many think that the school calendar should change. They say today's families have changed. But not everyone agrees. Some say a long rest is good for kids and adults. They feel summer is the best time for it.

Let's Look at the Opinions
MYTH AND HISTORY

As you read stories about the past, ask questions. Who says that story is true? How do we know? Is it based on facts? A story that seems to explain the past is sometimes called a **myth**. Myths sound good. They're easy to believe and repeat. Often, they have a little bit of truth. But they are not always based on facts. The second part of this chapter explained why the myth about summer break and farming is probably not true.

If someone uses a myth to support an opinion, it doesn't mean the opinion is wrong. Other information might support the opinion well. But a myth is not enough. Pay attention to facts. A story alone should not make up your mind.

When kids come back to school after a break, they might not remember everything they learned.

3

Does Year-Round School Help Kids Learn Better?

YES: Many Kids Learn Better in Year-Round School

In a traditional school, kids learn a lot between September and June. During the summer, they forget some of what they've learned. When school starts again, teachers spend weeks teaching things kids have forgotten.

For some, this isn't such a big problem. Students who have a lot of books at home can keep reading during the summer. Parents can help their kids keep learning. Kids who can go to camps and classes may not forget as much.

But many families can't afford summer camps and classes. Some parents can't help their kids keep learning. Kids whose parents don't speak English well might not get help practicing English at home. Some kids fall farther behind each summer. Others keep moving forward.

Helping Struggling Students

Year-round school might help struggling students. But it's hard to prove that it does. Each school is different. Each student is different, too. It can be hard to tell why some students learn more than others. But **researchers** are trying to find out.

Harris Cooper works at a college. He studied year-round schools. Cooper learned that year-round school doesn't help all students. But it does make a difference for some students. It helps three groups of kids most. The first is kids from low-income families. The second is those with learning disabilities. The third is those who are learning English.

Year-round school may help because students don't forget as much. Or it could be that the intersessions help students. During intersessions, kids who are having trouble can go to special classes. They can catch up. In a traditional school calendar, kids can catch up during summer school. But that's only once a year. In year-round school, teachers can help students sooner. They can keep kids from falling behind.

During intersessions, teachers can help students one at a time.

A school in North Carolina switched to a year-round calendar. The results were good. At the beginning of the next school year, students remembered more of what they had learned. "I wasn't expecting such a drastic change," said the principal. "And that was a surprise in a pleasant way."[2]

NO: Changing the Calendar Doesn't Help Kids Learn Better

It's true that kids may forget things over summer break. But they forget during short breaks, too. Paul von Hippel is an education **expert**. He says that year-round school and traditional school are about the same. Kids on traditional calendars forget a lot during the summer. But kids on year-round calendars forget a little during each intersession. Von Hippel says, "It is a bit like the race between tortoise and hare . . . except that, in this case, the race ends in a tie."[3]

Von Hippel says that at school, kids mostly have the same chances to learn. They have teachers, books, activities, and field trips. They all have a time and place to focus on learning. But at home, each kid is in a different **environment**. Some have more chances to learn than others. This isn't true only during summer vacation. It's true during weekends and intersession breaks, too.

Using School Time Well

Changing the calendar doesn't do much good. The time when breaks happen doesn't matter. But what happens at school matters. So does

Schools can set up field trips during breaks. This helps kids keep learning outside the classroom.

what happens during breaks. We shouldn't change the school calendar. Instead, we should make sure all students get the help they need during school. And we should find ways for all kids to keep learning during breaks. For example, schools could take kids on trips to museums and libraries during breaks. The calendar doesn't matter as much as how learning time is used.

Summing It Up!

Some people say students learn better in year-round school. But not everyone agrees. Changing how students are taught might be better than changing the calendar.

Let's Look at the Opinions

EXPERTS

Someone who knows a lot about a subject is called an expert. When you read about an expert, it may be easy to think they must be right. But experts often disagree with each other. How can that be?

Experts know a lot. But they form their opinions the same way the rest of us do. They look at a lot of facts. They learn as much as they can. Then they use what they know to choose their own opinions.

Facts are sometimes unclear. Experts can disagree about what they see. So don't base your opinion on what just one expert says. Find out what many experts think. And ask questions about their ideas.

Many water parks are open only during summer vacation.

4

Is Changing to Year-Round School Worth the Trouble?

NO: The Change Would Cause Too Many Problems

The school calendar is connected to all kinds of things, not just students. If the school calendar changed, there would have to be a lot of other changes, too. This wouldn't be worth the trouble.

Many businesses are set up to work with the traditional school calendar. Water parks and other businesses that make money only in summer would be hurt. Child-care centers and camps would have to make big changes. So would businesses that hire students in the summer.

Teachers and Parents Weigh In

Some teachers use the summer break to build their teaching skills. Without the long break, how would they do that? And what about teachers who take a second job during the summer? What would replace their income?

Changing calendars can also be frustrating for families who have children in more than one school. One parent in North Carolina agrees. She said, "It's inconvenient to have three kids on different schedules."[4]

Parents who work may have a hard time finding child care for a year-round calendar.

Some parents may dislike year-round calendars. They might even move away from towns with year-round schools. This could be a big problem if too many people moved away.

People could adjust to the change. But that would take a lot of time and energy. Year-round school doesn't do enough good to make that worthwhile. Research shows that calendars don't have much of an impact on learning. Other changes would improve kids' learning more than a change to the calendar would.

YES: Helping Struggling Students Is Worthwhile and Not Too Hard

Research shows that a year-round school calendar is better for kids who have a hard time learning. Helping all kids learn better should be schools' goal.

Kids learn better when teachers have more time to help. Some people say year-round schedules make better use of school time.

DID YOU KNOW?

US elementary students have an average of about 940 hours of classroom time each year. This puts the United States near the top compared with other countries. The highest is Chile, with about 1,010 hours. The lowest is Russia, with about 470 hours.

David Markward is a **superintendent** in Illinois. Schools in his town have started using a year-round calendar. He believes the change is worth it. "We have many students who struggle," he said.[5] He thinks year-round schools give them a better chance of success.

Change Doesn't Have to Be Hard

A year-round school calendar sounds like a big change. However, there are still plenty of breaks.

Kids spend a lot of time in school. Some say year-round school helps kids learn more in the same amount of time.

Some people call it a balanced calendar. In year-round school, school time is balanced. It is spread out evenly. In the traditional calendar, there are nine months full of school and then three months with no school at all.

In the long run, a balanced calendar could be good for everyone. Businesses, camps, and families can adjust to the change. They might discover that the new way is even better. The change will be worth the effort, because a balanced calendar makes sure that all kids have a chance to learn.

Summing It Up!

Changing school calendars would affect many people. Some people think it would cause too much trouble for teachers, parents, and businesses. But others think the change would not be so hard and would help many kids.

Let's Look at the Opinions

NAMING

Which sounds better to you, "year-round school" or a "balanced calendar"? People can try to change your opinion about something just by calling it by a different name! Pay attention when people use different words to talk about the same thing. Sometimes giving something a new name is useful. It can help readers understand what you're saying in a new way. But sometimes writers rename things just to change how you feel. The new name might not have facts behind it.

When you notice a name that sounds great or terrible, ask yourself, "What does that really mean?" For example, does year-round school mean going to school every day of the year?

Write What You Think!

The author shares different opinions in this book. Some opinions state why year-round school is good for students. Other opinions argue that changing the calendar doesn't help. It's important to know many sides of an argument before you form your own opinion.

Opinion writing has a purpose. The writer tries to convince the reader to agree with his or her point of view through different writing methods. One method is to use myth and history. Another method is to refer to the endorsement of an expert or a well-known person. Yet another method is to use different names for the same topic. All these methods help make a stronger point.

In writing your own opinion piece, here are six steps to follow:

Step One: *Choose what to write about.*

Pick a subject that interests you. Now think of a question you have about that subject. Decide how you would answer the question. Which side are you on?

Step Two: *Find out more.*

Before you write, find out more about your subject. Read what other people have to say. You could look for research. In this book, a researcher studied many different year-round schools and reported the results. Find out the facts. See if an expert has something to say on the subject.

Step Three: *State your opinion.*

The first few sentences should say what your paper is about. You may want to include a question. For example, you could start this way: "This essay is about year-round school. It asks the question, Is year-round school good for students?"

Next, write down your opinion. You can use phrases such as *I think, I believe,* or *in my opinion.* Examples are:

- "I think year-round school helps students learn."
- "I believe schools should keep the traditional calendar."
- "In my opinion, there are many benefits to year-round school."

Step Four: *Give reasons.*

Opinions should be followed up with reasons for those opinions. When reasons are logical, they influence others to think like you. Come up with two or three reasons why you think the way you do about your subject. Write each reason in a sentence. Use linking words like *because, since,* and *therefore* to connect your opinion with the reasons why you came to a certain conclusion. For example, if you are writing a piece on whether students should have year-round school, you might give these reasons:

- I think changing the school calendar is important, *since* students who are struggling will have better chances to learn.
- I think the school calendar should not change *because* then parents will not have to worry about taking more time off work.

Step Five: *Support your reasons.*

The opinion of a famous person or an authority is a good way to back up your reason. So are results from a survey or research study. Here is an example of how to do this:

First, give an opinion with a reason:

- I think changing the school calendar is important, *since* students who are struggling will have better chances to learn.

Then, give a fact to back up the reason:

- A school superintendent in Illinois agrees. He said it's worth making a change because it helps kids who have a hard time in school.

Step Six: *Write the ending.*

Summarize your opinion in the last sentence or two. This makes it clear for the reader what side you are on and why you think the way you do. A good summary wraps up your argument and helps convince the reader to think as you do. You could begin the last sentence with any of these phrases, or you can think of your own:

- For all these reasons, . . .
- As the research indicates, . . .
- To sum up, . . .

GLOSSARY

enrichment (en-RICH-ment): Extra learning.

environment (en-VIE-ron-ment): The place where a student spends time. The nearby people, things, and activities.

expert (EX-pert): A person who knows a lot about a subject.

intersessions (IN-ter-SESH-uns): The times between school terms.

myth (MITH): A story that many people believe, but that may not be true.

researchers (RE-surch-urs): People who look into a subject carefully.

superintendent (soo-per-in-TEN-dent): A person in charge of the schools in an area.

terms (TURMS): Periods of time.

tradition (truh-DISH-un): An important habit repeated over many years.

BIBLIOGRAPHY

Books

Palmer, Erin. *Summer School, Yes or No*. Vero Beach, FL: Rourke Educational, 2016.

Pelleschi, Andrea. *Olivia and Oscar Build an Opinion Piece*. Chicago, IL: Norwood House, 2014.

Websites

Common Questions about Year-Round Education
http://nayre.org/questions.html

Research Spotlight on Year-Round Education
http://www.nea.org/tools/17057.htm

SOURCE NOTES

1. Jo Ann Barton. "Year-Round Schooling Helps Struggling Students to Achieve." *At Issue: Year-Round Schools*. Detroit, MI: Thomson Gale, 2008. Print. 60.

2. Elise Franco. "Year-Round School Shows Signs of Success." *Shelby Star*. Shelby Star, 3 Aug. 2017. Web. 15 Feb. 2018.

3. Chris Weller. "Year-Round School Is Booming—But Its Benefits Are Over-Hyped." *Business Insider*. 5 June 2017. Web. 15 Feb. 2018.

4. Alan Dessoff. "Is Year-Round Schooling on Track?" *District Administration*. District Administration, 1 July 2011. Web. 15 Feb. 2018.

5. Jo Ann Barton. "Year-Round Schooling Helps Struggling Students to Achieve." *At Issue: Year-Round Schools*. Detroit, MI: Thomson Gale, 2008. Print. 60.

Index

About the Author

Carolyn Williams-Noren writes poems and essays for adults, as well as books for students. She enjoys hearing kids' ideas about big questions. She lives in Minneapolis with her husband and two daughters.